CHRISTMAS
COUPON

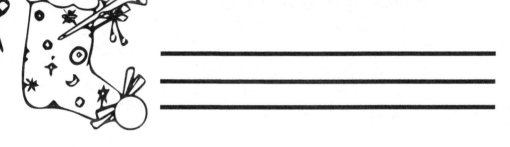

_____

_____

_____

FROM : _____

TO : _____

DATE : _____

TERMS
CAN BE REDEEMED ONLY ONCE

EXPIRES : IN 12 MONTHS

CHRISTMAS COUPON

_____

_____

_____

FROM : _____

TO : _____

DATE : _____

EXPIRES : IN 12 MONTHS

TERMS

CAN BE REDEEMED
ONLY ONCE

CHRISTMAS
COUPON

FROM

TO

DATE

EXPIRES : IN 12 MONTHS

TERMS

CHRISTMAS COUPON

_____

_____

_____

FROM : _____

TO : _____

DATE : _____

EXPIRES : IN 12 MONTHS

TERMS
CAN BE REDEEMED
ONLY ONCE

CHRISTMAS COUPON

_____

_____

_____

FROM : _____

TO : _____

DATE : _____

EXPIRES : IN 12 MONTHS

TERMS
CAN BE REDEEMED
ONLY ONCE

CHRISTMAS COUPON

FROM

TO

DATE

EXPIRES : IN 12 MONTHS

CHRISTMAS COUPON

_____

_____

_____

FROM : _____

TO : _____

DATE : _____

EXPIRES : IN 12 MONTHS

TERMS
CAN BE REDEEMED
ONLY ONCE

CHRISTMAS
COUPON

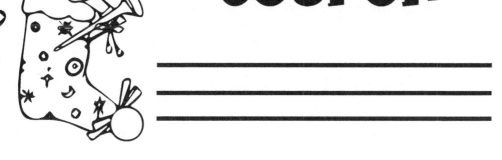

_____

_____

_____

FROM : _____

TO : _____

DATE : _____

EXPIRES : IN 12 MONTHS

TERMS
CAN BE REDEEMED
ONLY ONCE

CHRISTMAS
COUPON

FROM : _____

TO : _____

DATE : _____

EXPIRES : IN 12 MONTHS

TERMS
CAN BE REDEEMED
ONLY ONCE

CHRISTMAS
COUPON

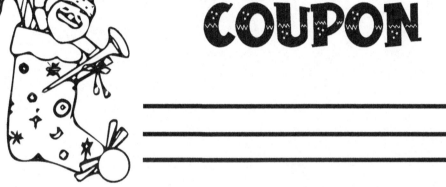

—————————————

—————————————

—————————————

FROM : ———————————————

TO : ———————————————

DATE : ———————————————

EXPIRES : IN 12 MONTHS

TERMS
CAN BE REDEEMED
ONLY ONCE

CHRISTMAS
COUPON

FROM:

TO:

DATE:

EXPIRES : IN 12 MONTHS

TERMS

CHRISTMAS
COUPON

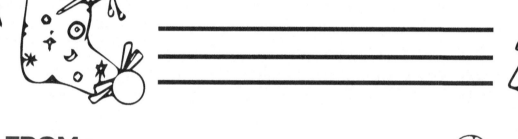

_____

_____

_____

FROM : _____

TO : _____

DATE : _____

EXPIRES : IN 12 MONTHS

TERMS
CAN BE REDEEMED
ONLY ONCE

CHRISTMAS
COUPON

_____

_____

_____

FROM : _____

TO : _____

DATE : _____

EXPIRES : IN 12 MONTHS

TERMS
CAN BE REDEEMED
ONLY ONCE

CHRISTMAS COUPON

_____

_____

_____

FROM : _____

TO : _____

DATE : _____

EXPIRES : IN 12 MONTHS

TERMS
CAN BE REDEEMED
ONLY ONCE

CHRISTMAS
COUPON

FROM :

TO :

DATE :

TERMS
CAN BE REDEEMED
ONLY ONCE

EXPIRES : IN 12 MONTHS

CHRISTMAS
COUPON

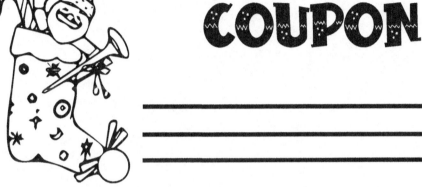

_____

_____

_____

FROM : _____

TO : _____

DATE : _____

EXPIRES : IN 12 MONTHS

TERMS
CAN BE REDEEMED
ONLY ONCE

CHRISTMAS COUPON

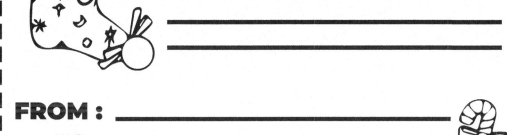

_____
_____
_____

FROM : _____
TO : _____
DATE : _____

EXPIRES : IN 12 MONTHS

TERMS
CAN BE REDEEMED
ONLY ONCE

CHRISTMAS COUPON

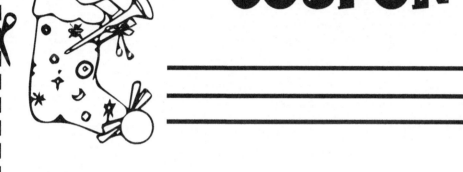

——————————————————

——————————————————

——————————————————

FROM : ——————————————

TO : ——————————————

DATE : ——————————————

EXPIRES : IN 12 MONTHS

TERMS
CAN BE REDEEMED
ONLY ONCE

CHRISTMAS
COUPON

FROM

TO

DATE :

EXPIRES : IN 12 MONTHS

TERMS

CHRISTMAS COUPON

_____

_____

_____

FROM : _____

TO : _____

DATE : _____

EXPIRES : IN 12 MONTHS

TERMS
CAN BE REDEEMED
ONLY ONCE

CHRISTMAS COUPON

FROM :

TO :

DATE :

EXPIRES IN 12 MONTHS

TERMS
CAN BE REDEEMED
ONE TIME

CHRISTMAS
COUPON

_____

_____

_____

FROM : _____

TO : _____

DATE : _____

EXPIRES : IN 12 MONTHS

TERMS
CAN BE REDEEMED
ONLY ONCE

CHRISTMAS

COUPON

CHRISTMAS COUPON

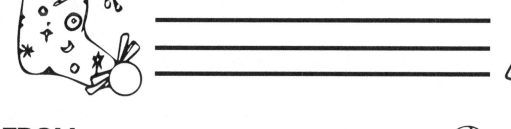

_____

_____

_____

FROM : _____

TO : _____

DATE : _____

EXPIRES : IN 12 MONTHS

TERMS
CAN BE REDEEMED ONLY ONCE

CHRISTMAS
COUPON

FROM :

TO :

DATE :

EXPIRES : IN 12 MONTHS

TERMS
CAN BE TRANSFERRED
ONE PER USE

CHRISTMAS COUPON

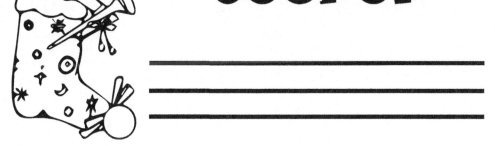

_____

_____

_____

FROM : _____

TO : _____

DATE : _____

EXPIRES : IN 12 MONTHS

TERMS

CAN BE REDEEMED
ONLY ONCE

CHRISTMAS
COUPON

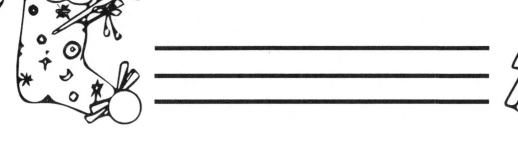

_____

_____

_____

FROM : _____

TO : _____

DATE : _____

EXPIRES : IN 12 MONTHS

TERMS

CAN BE REDEEMED
ONLY ONCE

CHRISTMAS
COUPON

_____

_____

_____

FROM : _____

TO : _____

DATE : _____

EXPIRES : IN 12 MONTHS

TERMS
CAN BE REDEEMED
ONLY ONCE

CHRISTMAS COUPON

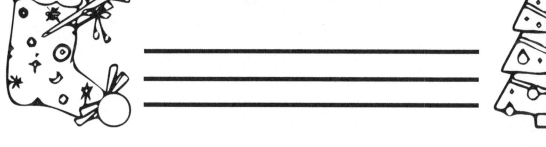

_____

_____

_____

FROM : _____

TO : _____

DATE : _____

EXPIRES : IN 12 MONTHS

TERMS
CAN BE REDEEMED
ONLY ONCE

CHRISTMAS
COUPON

FROM:

TO:

DATE:

TERMS
CAN BE REDEEMED
ONLY ONCE

EXPIRES IN 12 MONTHS

CHRISTMAS
COUPON

_____

_____

_____

FROM : _____

TO : _____

DATE : _____

TERMS
CAN BE REDEEMED
ONLY ONCE

EXPIRES : IN 12 MONTHS

CHRISTMAS
COUPON

TERMS
CAN BE REDEEMED
ONLY ONCE

FROM:
TO:
DATE:

EXPIRES - IN 12 MONTHS

CHRISTMAS
COUPON

_____

_____

_____

FROM : _____

TO : _____

DATE : _____

EXPIRES : IN 12 MONTHS

TERMS
CAN BE REDEEMED
ONLY ONCE

CHRISTMAS
COUPON

FROM :

TO :

DATE :

EXPIRES : IN 12 MONTHS

TERMS
CAN BE REDEEMED
ONLY ONCE

CHRISTMAS
COUPON

_____

_____

_____

FROM : _____

TO : _____

DATE : _____

EXPIRES : IN 12 MONTHS

TERMS
CAN BE REDEEMED
ONLY ONCE

CHRISTMAS COUPON

_____
_____
_____

FROM : _____

TO : _____

DATE : _____

EXPIRES : IN 12 MONTHS

CHRISTMAS COUPON

FROM :

TO :

DATE :

EXPIRES IN 12 MONTHS

TERMS
CAN BE REDEEMED
ONLY ONCE

CHRISTMAS
COUPON

_____

_____

_____

FROM : _____

TO : _____

DATE : _____

EXPIRES : IN 12 MONTHS

TERMS
CAN BE REDEEMED
ONLY ONCE

CHRISTMAS
COUPON

————————————————

————————————————

————————————————

FROM : ————————————————

TO : ————————————————

DATE : ————————————————

EXPIRES : IN 12 MONTHS

TERMS
CAN BE REDEEMED
ONLY ONCE

CHRISTMAS
COUPON

FROM

TO

DATE

EXPIRES IN __ MONTHS

TERMS
CAN BE MODIFIED
ONLY ONCE

CHRISTMAS
COUPON

_____

_____

_____

FROM : _____

TO : _____

DATE : _____

EXPIRES : IN 12 MONTHS

TERMS
CAN BE REDEEMED
ONLY ONCE

CHRISTMAS
COUPON

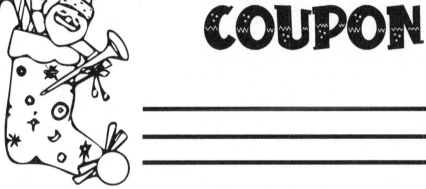

_____
_____
_____

FROM : _____

TO : _____

DATE : _____

EXPIRES : IN 12 MONTHS

TERMS
CAN BE REDEEMED
ONLY ONCE

CHRISTMAS
COUPON

FROM:

TO:

DATE:

EXPIRES : IN 12 MONTHS

TERMS
CAN BE REDEEMED
ONLY ONCE

CHRISTMAS
COUPON

_____

_____

_____

FROM : _____

TO : _____

DATE : _____

EXPIRES : IN 12 MONTHS

TERMS
CAN BE REDEEMED
ONLY ONCE

CHRISTMAS
COUPON

FROM:
TO:
DATE:

TERMS
CAN BE REDEEMED
ONLY ONCE

EXPIRES : IN 12 MONTHS

CHRISTMAS
COUPON

_____

_____

_____

FROM : _____

TO : _____

DATE : _____

EXPIRES : IN 12 MONTHS

TERMS
CAN BE REDEEMED
ONLY ONCE

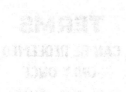

CHRISTMAS
COUPON

FROM :

TO :

DATE :

EXPIRES IN 12 MONTHS

TERMS
CAN BE TRADED TO
GIFT GIVER

CHRISTMAS
COUPON

———————————————
———————————————
———————————————

FROM : _____

TO : _____

DATE : _____

EXPIRES : IN 12 MONTHS

TERMS
CAN BE REDEEMED
ONLY ONCE

CHRISTMAS

COUPON

FROM:

TO:

DATE:

EXPIRES:

TERMS

CHRISTMAS COUPON

_____

_____

_____

FROM : _____

TO : _____

DATE : _____

EXPIRES : IN 12 MONTHS

TERMS

CAN BE REDEEMED
ONLY ONCE

CHRISTMAS
COUPON

FROM

TO

DATE

EXPIRES IN 12 MONTHS

TERMS
CAN BE REDEEMED
ONLY ONCE

CHRISTMAS
COUPON

_____
_____
_____

FROM : _____

TO : _____

DATE : _____

EXPIRES : IN 12 MONTHS

TERMS
CAN BE REDEEMED ONLY ONCE

CHRISTMAS COUPON

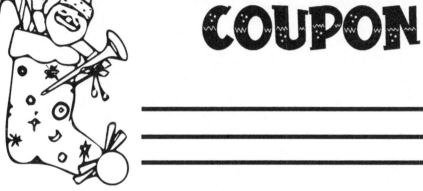

_____

_____

_____

FROM : _____

TO : _____

DATE : _____

EXPIRES : IN 12 MONTHS

TERMS

CAN BE REDEEMED
ONLY ONCE

CHRISTMAS
COUPON

FROM:

TO:

DATE:

TERMS

EXPIRES IN 12 MONTHS

CHRISTMAS
COUPON

_____

_____

_____

FROM : _____

TO : _____

DATE : _____

EXPIRES : IN 12 MONTHS

TERMS
CAN BE REDEEMED
ONLY ONCE

CHRISTMAS COUPON

_____

_____

_____

FROM : _____

TO : _____

DATE : _____

EXPIRES : IN 12 MONTHS

TERMS

CAN BE REDEEMED ONLY ONCE

CHRISTMAS COUPON

_____

_____

_____

FROM : _____

TO : _____

DATE : _____

EXPIRES : IN 12 MONTHS

TERMS
CAN BE REDEEMED
ONLY ONCE

CHRISTMAS
COUPON

FROM:
TO:
DATE:

TERMS

EXPIRES IN 12 MONTHS

CHRISTMAS COUPON

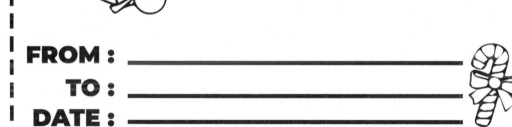

——————————————
——————————————
——————————————

FROM : _____
TO : _____
DATE : _____

EXPIRES : IN 12 MONTHS

TERMS
CAN BE REDEEMED
ONLY ONCE

CHRISTMAS
COUPON

FROM :

TO :

DATE :

EXPIRES : IN 12 MONTHS

TERMS

CHRISTMAS
COUPON

_____
_____
_____

FROM : _____
TO : _____
DATE : _____

EXPIRES : IN 12 MONTHS

TERMS
CAN BE REDEEMED
ONLY ONCE

CHRISTMAS COUPON

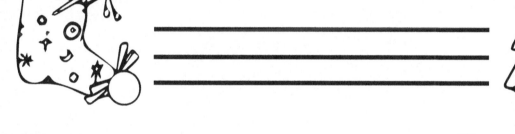

_____

_____

_____

FROM : _____

TO : _____

DATE : _____

EXPIRES : IN 12 MONTHS

TERMS
CAN BE REDEEMED
ONLY ONCE

CHRISTMAS COUPON

FROM : _____

TO : _____

DATE : _____

EXPIRES : TIP 12 MONTHS

TERMS

CAN BE REDEEMED
ONLY ONE

CHRISTMAS
COUPON

———————————————
———————————————
———————————————

FROM : ———————————————
TO : ———————————————
DATE : ———————————————

TERMS
CAN BE REDEEMED
ONLY ONCE

EXPIRES : IN 12 MONTHS

CHRISTMAS COUPON

_____

_____

_____

FROM : _____

TO : _____

DATE : _____

EXPIRES : IN 12 MONTHS

TERMS

CAN BE REDEEMED
ONLY ONCE

CHRISTMAS
COUPON

_____
_____
_____

FROM : _____

TO : _____

DATE : _____

EXPIRES : IN 12 MONTHS

TERMS
CAN BE REDEEMED
ONLY ONCE

CHRISTMAS
COUPON

_____
_____
_____

FROM : _____
TO : _____
DATE : _____

EXPIRES : IN 12 MONTHS

TERMS
CAN BE REDEEMED
ONLY ONCE

CHRISTMAS
COUPON

_____

_____

_____

FROM : _____

TO : _____

DATE : _____

EXPIRES : IN 12 MONTHS

TERMS
CAN BE REDEEMED
ONLY ONCE

CHRISTMAS
COUPON

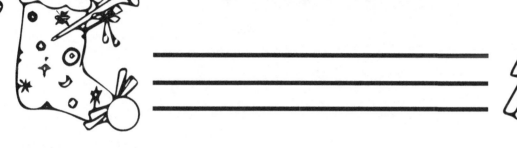

_____

_____

_____

FROM : _____

TO : _____

DATE : _____

EXPIRES : IN 12 MONTHS

TERMS
CAN BE REDEEMED
ONLY ONCE

CHRISTMAS
COUPON

FROM:

TO:

DATE:

EXPIRES IN 72 MONTHS

TERMS
CAN BE USED FOR
ONLY ONE

CHRISTMAS
COUPON

————————————————
————————————————
————————————————

FROM : ————————————————

TO : ————————————————

DATE : ————————————————

EXPIRES : IN 12 MONTHS

TERMS
CAN BE REDEEMED
ONLY ONCE

CHRISTMAS COUPON

FROM:

TO:

DATE:

EXPIRES : IN 12 MONTHS

TERMS
CAN BE REDEEMED
ONLY ONCE

CHRISTMAS
COUPON

_____

_____

_____

FROM : _____

TO : _____

DATE : _____

EXPIRES : IN 12 MONTHS

TERMS
**CAN BE REDEEMED
ONLY ONCE**

CHRISTMAS
COUPON

FROM :

TO :

DATE :

EXPIRES : IN 12 MONTHS

TERMS
CAN BE REDEEMED
ONLY ONCE

CHRISTMAS COUPON

_____

_____

_____

FROM : _____

TO : _____

DATE : _____

EXPIRES : IN 12 MONTHS

TERMS
CAN BE REDEEMED
ONLY ONCE

CHRISTMAS COUPON

_____

_____

_____

FROM : _____

TO : _____

DATE : _____

EXPIRES : IN 12 MONTHS

TERMS
CAN BE REDEEMED
ONLY ONCE

CHRISTMAS
COUPON

TERMS
CAN-BE STOPPED
ONLY ONCE

FROM :
TO :
DATE :

EXPIRES : IN 12 MONTHS

CHRISTMAS
COUPON

_____

_____

_____

FROM : _____

TO : _____

DATE : _____

EXPIRES : IN 12 MONTHS

TERMS
CAN BE REDEEMED
ONLY ONCE

CHRISTMAS
COUPON

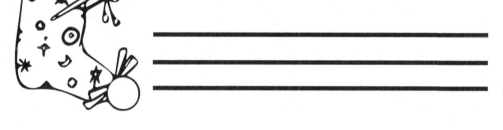

_____

_____

_____

FROM : _____

TO : _____

DATE : _____

EXPIRES : IN 12 MONTHS

TERMS

CAN BE REDEEMED
ONLY ONCE

CHRISTMAS
COUPON

FROM:

TO:

DATE:

EXPIRES IN 12 MONTHS

TERMS
CAN BE REDEEMED
ONLY ONCE

CHRISTMAS
COUPON

_____

_____

_____

FROM : _____

TO : _____

DATE : _____

EXPIRES : IN 12 MONTHS

TERMS
CAN BE REDEEMED
ONLY ONCE

CHRISTMAS
COUPON

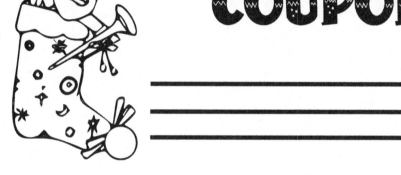

_____

_____

_____

FROM : _____

TO : _____

DATE : _____

EXPIRES : IN 12 MONTHS

TERMS
CAN BE REDEEMED
ONLY ONCE

CHRISTMAS COUPON

FROM :

TO :

DATE :

EXPIRES : IN 12 MONTHS

TERMS
CAN BE REDEEMED
ONLY ONCE

CHRISTMAS
COUPON

_____

_____

_____

FROM : _____

TO : _____

DATE : _____

EXPIRES : IN 12 MONTHS

TERMS
CAN BE REDEEMED
ONLY ONCE

Made in the USA
Monee, IL
25 October 2024